YOUNG POCAHONTAS

IN THE INDIAN WORLD

Helen C. Rountree

ISBN 0-9648727-0-6

Printed by
J & R Graphic Services, Inc.
124 Production Dr.
Yorktown, Virginia 23693

Order Form Located In Back of Book

Grateful thanks go to the staff of Jamestown Settlement, A Living History Museum. These friends facilitated the author's taking of many of the photographs and posed in costume for some of them. Thanks especially to Erik Holland (sitting in village scene), Anastasia Bergh (carrying firewood, cooking food), Henry Bond and Karen Aneiro (canoeing), Terry Bond and Mila Gaetano (curing scene), Mila again (cordage-making, holding cradleboard), Tina Gutshall (pottery-making) and Frank Hardister and Kevin Garland (fort scene).

Jennifer Riley and Jean Hager were kind enough to lend their elementary education expertise in reviewing the text.

See order form on last page.

TABLE OF CONTENTS

CHAPTER ONE
BACKGROUND

Many people have heard the legend of Pocahontas, the Virginia Indian "princess." She is usually shown as a tall, beautiful young woman. She supposedly saved Captain John Smith when her father wanted to kill him, and then, because of her love for him, she went on to save the English colony at Jamestown from starving to death. Many people also think she later married John Smith. All of these romantic ideas are incorrect. The reality was rather different. Among other things, when Pocahontas met John Smith, she was eleven or twelve years old and he was

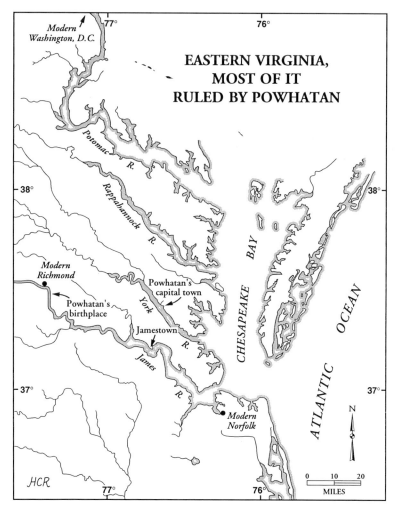

twenty-seven. They were fond of each other, but there was never a romance between them. It was another Englishman that she fell in love with and married.

Pocahontas was the daughter of a powerful Indian chief. She was also the child of divorced parents. She spent her early years with her mother, and later she went to live with her father. The divorce meant that Pocahontas had no full brothers or sisters, but because her father married many times and had many children, she had dozens of half-sisters and -brothers.

Pocahontas's father was Powhatan (poh-HAH-tan)*, who ruled most of eastern Virginia. It was the custom in his world for a ruler to marry many wives from the different parts of his domain. We do not know where Pocahontas's mother came from, but she was definitely a Native American, not a European. We also do not know the mother's name, for no English colonist ever wrote it down. But when Powhatan visited her village one day, he chose her from among all the girls, probably because she was handsome and lively. (Pocahontas would turn out the same way, although she never grew very tall.)

Powhatan then married her and took her home to his capital town on the York River. There she lived with him and several of his other wives until Pocahontas was born. Then custom demanded that Powhatan separate from her, sending her and the baby back to her family, while he married another wife. He had to treat all his wives like that, even the ones he fell in love with. But that kind of separation and divorce could be friendly, since everyone knew that the marriage was only for a few years, not forever.

---

* But modern Virginians say POW-a-tan.

CHAPTER TWO

POCAHONTAS'S EARLY YEARS

Pocahontas's earliest memories were of her parents after their separation. But far from being a lonely child of separated parents, Pocahontas was never alone.

Indian village scene

She lived in a village with her mother, her maternal grandparents, her mother's unmarried sisters (who moved away when they married), and her mother's brothers and their wives and children. She probably also saw her father from time to time, for visiting relatives was an Indian custom. The ties between kinsmen were very, very strong in the Indian world.

Pocahontas was not called by that name in her early years. Soon after she was born, her parents gave her the name Amonute (ah-moh-NOO-tay). Everyone called her that, unless they made up nicknames for her. She was also given a secret, very personal name: Matoaka (mah-TOH-kah). She never told anyone her secret name until she went to live among the English and took the English name of Rebecca.

In the early months of her life, Pocahontas spent most of her time on a cradleboard. She would be bathed in the river each morning — no matter how cold it was — and then bound to the board with deerskin thongs. She was not wrapped very warmly, either. The bath and the limited wrapping were meant to make her hardy. Indian parents seldom felt the cold; mothers and fathers both had to be strong and able to endure all weathers, because they worked outdoors most of the time.

Pocahontas in her cradleboard went wherever her mother went in those days.

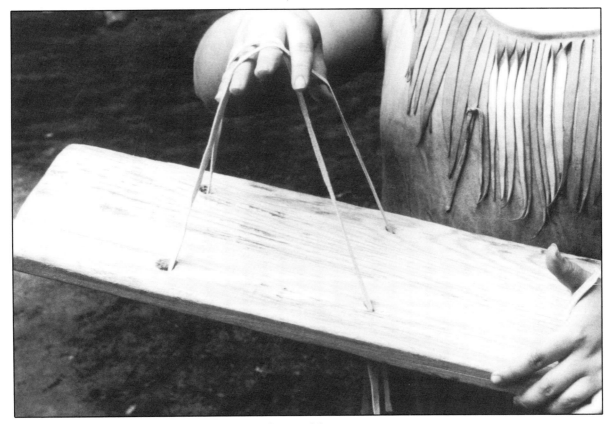

What a Powhatan Indian cradleboard was like

And that meant going a lot of places, for all Indian mothers were working mothers. Later Pocahontas would spend her days learning to work, too; lazy people were not accepted in her world. So as a baby, Pocahontas was taken out in the fields, woods, rivers, and marshes, all the places women's work took them. She saw all these things from her secure place on the cradleboard. The cradleboard was also her bed at night — no fear of falling out of it. Of course, several times a day she had to be taken off the cradleboard to be cleaned up and her diaper of moss changed. Later she would also be allowed the freedom to crawl and then toddle around the village, while her older cousins watched over her.

The house that Pocahontas grew up in was built by her mother and the other women. Its framework was made of tree saplings and then covered with mats made of reeds from the marshes. The mats wore out in a few months, letting the rain

Indian longhouse, with woman bringing in firewood for the cooking fire

come in. So Indian women spent a lot of time — when they were home — making new mats. An Indian house could be built in a day or so by several women and their children working together. Like so many other jobs in the Indian world, house-building needed the joint efforts of a group of people. And when several people were doing it, work became a social or fun event rather than just work.

The finished house had a high, rounded ceiling, with room to store things over people's heads. There was a central fire, which had to be kept going all the time or else it was bad luck. The smoke filled the upper part of the house and then went out through a hole left in the roof. Pocahontas grew up sleeping in a cloud of wood smoke!

The lower, living area of the house had a central aisle flanked with built-in wooden platforms. These platforms were covered with mats, deerskins, or fur rugs; they served as benches to sit on or beds to sleep on. Her mother slept alone, with Pocahontas on her cradleboard nearby. The married couples in the family got some privacy by putting up a

Interior of Indian house, with built-in beds along the wall

wall of mats around their sleeping area. There was no bathroom. The villagers bathed in the river and used the woods at the edge of the village as a toilet.

Houses were rather dark places, even in the daytime. The only light came from the smokehole, the central fire, and the one or two low doors (everyone had to crawl through them). That is why Indian people did so much of their work outdoors where the light was better, even if the weather was cold. It took a rainy day or a very, very cold one to make people work indoors.

Pocahontas's mother probably nursed her for at least two years, before starting her on other food. The Indians did not have baby formula or bottles. In an emergency, they could feed babies "walnut milk," which was crushed nuts mixed with water. But that drink was considered a luxury food for adults most of the time. Pocahontas's people did not drink milk after infancy because they had no cows.

When Pocahontas began eating regular food, it was food that was partly familiar to us. Cornbread is something the Indians taught the English to make. There were also stews with vegetables — garden ones or wild ones — and meat. All of the meat came from wild animals: deer, bear, beaver, raccoon, opossum, squirrel, and rabbit. (Pocahontas did not usually make these animals into pets in real life; she and her family ate them instead.) Oysters, mussels and clams were sometimes added to the stew, as well as berries in season. Fish, oysters and deer meat were also roasted, sometimes slowly enough that they were smoked in the process. Yet there was one food that we eat but the Indians did not: onions. Pocahontas's people did not think onions were fit to eat.

Pocahontas's family did not have regular mealtimes; they ate when they were hungry. That is why the family always kept a stewpot boiling on a fire in the yard. People added water, vegetables, meat, and cornbread dumplings to it during the

Food being cooked, Indian-style (though the old-fashioned stewpot would have been much bigger)

course of the day, depending on what work they had been doing. Dippers for stew or drinking water were made from turtle shells or large oyster shells. Dishes for roasted meat and baked cornbread were carved wooden platters, the food being eaten with the fingers. On special occasions at least, people washed their hands before eating. There were no tables or chairs in Pocahontas's village. People sat down to eat on mats spread on the ground.

Pocahontas was never alone. She was always with her relatives — playing with her cousins, helping her mother, aunts, and grandmother, and listening to the stories and songs of older men and women. In the evening the people of the village often danced; men and women of all ages loved dancing.

We don't know much about the games a little Indian girl would have played.

But Pocahontas and her cousins would have played some form of "tag." She would have had dolls, probably made from cornhusks. And the girls practiced doing grown-up things, like making pots and baskets, while the boys played with bows and arrows and tried out their hunting skills. All the children played in the water and around canoes. Both men and women had to know how to manage canoes in order to do their work.

Paddling a dugout canoe

As Pocahontas watched her mother and aunts and older cousins, she learned how to do a woman's work. She was allowed to learn at her own speed, as fast or slowly as she wanted. (Since she was bright, she probably learned fast.) There was no school for her to go to. Her people did not have writing, so she did not learn to read until much later, when she went to live among the English. The children in her world learned from the adults they watched. And watching and helping adults was the "cool" thing to do in a world where there were no computer games or TV. Everyone knew that people were supposed to be cooperative and helpful in the adult world. Men and boys were expected to be good fighters — but only toward outsiders, not toward their own people.

Pocahontas's days were varied during her girlhood; there was no one typical day. There were so many different, time-consuming things that hard-working mothers did that each day brought somewhat different jobs. And some jobs were seasonal, too. The Indians in eastern Virginia had a year with five seasons in it. So let us see what Pocahontas would have been doing on a fictional day in each of those seasons, say, in 1601 when she was about six years old and still living with her mother.

Sun low over a tidal river in Virginia

CHAPTER THREE
A GIRL'S DAY IN SPRING

On a chilly day in spring, when the trees were newly green, Pocahontas and her family went down to the river near their village and bathed as dawn was breaking. The water was very cold still, but they bathed in it anyway. They rubbed themselves briskly, for they had no soap or shampoo. Afterward, as the sun rose, they prayed, offered bits of tobacco, and gave thanks for another day.

After the icy cold bath, the chilly air felt almost warm. (Later in the day, the sun would heat the air a bit more.) Men, women, and children wore few clothes even when it was cold. They stayed on the move and they also smeared bear's oil on their bare skin. Adults wore loincloths; children (even a chief's daughter like Pocahontas) wore nothing. People going into the woods added moccasins and leggings to protect against thorny briers and poison ivy. But most of their work outdoors required so much activity that warm deerskin capes would get in the way (the Indians did not make jackets like ours). So they toughed it out, bare-chested, and prided themselves on their endurance.

Pocahontas and her family returned home from the river and ate some left-over stew before going about the day's tasks. The smaller boys in the family got their breakfast only after some target practice: with their little bows and arrows they had to hit a piece of moss their mothers tossed into the air. They were learning early that men and boys who were good marksmen had more food to eat, as well as earning the approval of the women.

The refilling of the family stewpot on that early spring day was shared by everyone. Everybody had to go out from the village and get food (some Indian families left the village for days at a time at this season, in order to find enough food). Pocahontas's uncles and boy cousins took the canoe out into the river and visited their fish trap, which had shad and herring in it just then. While they did that,

Modern version of an Indian fish trap, with Great Blue Herons stealing the fish. The Indians would have made it with hedges of saplings and reeds.

some of Pocahontas's aunts fetched water from the nearby spring and poured it into the stewpot — it took several gallons. The last of the family's firewood supply started the water boiling. Meanwhile, Pocahontas and her girl cousins followed her mother to some old, unused fields a mile away through the woods. There they filled their carrying baskets with the wild greens that were just coming up — later these would be too bitter to eat. (Many of those greens will still grow in your yard if it is not mowed.) The plants went into the stewpot along with the fish the men brought home. Some of the boys had dived into the cold river for oysters and mussels. These were roasted now and eaten by anyone who was hungry.

Later the family members went out again. The supply of firewood had to be replenished, to cook more food and to keep people warm that night while they slept. So some aunts and older girl cousins went out for branches and logs. Pocahontas did not go with them. It was heavy labor that involved a long walk into the woods, and she was not yet old enough to be much help. The men and boys went out hunting, the men for deer and wild turkey and the boys for smaller animals. They were all good enough shots that they sometimes killed their prey immediately. But they were all prepared to run for miles after wounded animals if they had to; Indian men prided themselves on being very fast cross-country runners. The men who went after turkeys took the dogs with them. Indian dogs were not pets. They were hunting dogs who lived in scraps. They were rather small — about the size of a beagle — and they howled instead of barking.

Pocahontas's mother took her and a couple of aunts and the younger girl and boy cousins out in the canoe to gather tuckahoe roots that afternoon, when the tide happened to be low. Before they left, they prayed and made an offering of tobacco. They needed to do this. The rivers and creeks in eastern Virginia were (and are) quite wide.

Typical wide tidal river: the James, from the south end of Jamestown Island

Thunderstorms can come up quickly on spring afternoons. As you know, it is very

Thunderstorm blowing down a tidal river (the Rappahannock in this case)

dangerous to be out on a river during a thunderstorm. On a wide waterway, the wind can whip up high waves that can sink the boat; the boat can also be hit by lightning. So Pocahontas and her relatives prayed that no storm would come up until they had finished their work and come home safely.

They all climbed into the family canoe and paddled up the river and into a creek with many curves.

Pine and oak trees lined its banks for a long way. King-fishers were diving into the shallow water, and herons and egrets were stalking slowly around, which is their way of finding fish. Finally the canoe arrived at a wide marsh in one of the curves of the creek.

Tuckahoe plants grow in freshwater marshes and have leaves that are shaped like arrowheads. They are still very common in Virginia. They have roots, down in the mud, that are much like potatoes except that they can sting your mouth if you eat them

When paddling up a tidal creek, trees and birds come alive.

raw. These roots were a big part of the Virginia Indian people's diet in the spring, when last summer's corn and last fall's nuts had run out. So Pocahontas and her relatives had to go out and dig lots of tuckahoe every few days.

The women rapidly dug up the roots and tossed them out into the stream; the work was very hard, but the women were very strong. The children, who were wading around, caught the roots, washed the mud off

Marshy freshwater creek, with one kind of Tuckahoe (Arrow Arum) growing in it

them, and put them into the canoe. When a big load had accumulated, Pocahontas and her relatives paddled home; that was hard work, too, in a heavy wooden canoe loaded with both "potatoes" and people.

Back at the village, the afternoon's catch of animals had gone into the stewpot, after first being skinned. One uncle had brought in a deer, and his wife would begin tanning the hide the next day, before making clothes for both of them.

Some of the other women dealt with the tuckahoe, peeling off its rind and cutting it into thin slices for sun-drying the next day. Once it was sun-dried, people could eat it without stinging their mouths. Two of Pocahontas's aunts took the end of the previous batch of tuckahoe and pounded it to flour in wooden mortars. Then they added water to the flour to make dumplings, and these went into the stewpot.

At sunset the family stopped work and prayed and offered tobacco again, giving thanks for a successful day of getting food. Spring could be a hungry time for the Indians. But Pocahontas's mother's family had many expert hands to get food for everyone. When people were not eating, they were visiting and telling stories while watching the tiny children let out of their cradleboards. Some of the adults and older children had enough energy left to get up a community dance in the center of the village. But the night had not gone too far before, one by one or two by two, everybody had gone into the house, shut the doors, and gone to bed. This was the really warm time of day for Pocahontas. The house had a good fire, and she slept under a deerskin blanket with some of her girl cousins. It was very cozy.

CHAPTER FOUR
A GIRL'S DAY IN EARLY SUMMER

On a warm day in early summer, which was the planting season, Pocahontas and her family got up before dawn as usual. The bath in the river was pleasantly cool. The prayers said before the sun became hot were heartfelt, for the people needed a good crop of corn that summer. After those who were hungry had snacked from the stewpot, the family members all went together to plant corn in a large field.

Usually it was only the women who worked at raising corn and beans, while the men hunted and fished for their families and raised the tobacco. But today the men were going along, too, for everyone worked together in the field they planted each year for the great chief, Pocahontas's father. The care of the chief's field was the only work that Pocahontas's uncles shared with her mother and aunts. At all other times, men's work and women's work were separate things. But both kinds of work were important, so that men and women respected each other for what they did.

Among the Virginia Indians, every family had at least four fields in operation each year. Because the soil "wore out," the older fields grew less and less corn each year. So the Indians had shift from field to field. The women planted a new field (number-one), a field that had been new last year (number-two), and a field that had been new two years ago (number-three). Meanwhile, the men were clearing a brand-new field this year by de-barking the trees to make them die. Early next spring they would burn them, making that year's new field, which the women would use as number-one. This year's number-one field would become number-two; this year's number-two field would become number-three; and they would stop planting the oldest field (this year's number-three) and gather the wild greens growing up in it instead. People were always thinking ahead and preparing for the next year.

This year:

Clearing new field	Field #1	Field #2	Field #3

Next year:

Clearing new field	Field #1	Field #2	Field #3	Old field

Pocahontas's mother and aunts had planted number-one field two months ago, so its corn would be ripe (if there was enough rain) in what we call August. Except for weeding it, which they would do the next day, that field could be left alone. Already the corn was three feet high, and the beans planted with it had begun to twine themselves around the cornstalks. Number-two field had been planted nearly a month before; its corn would be ripe in what we call Septem-

Corn stalks, with beans twining around them

ber. In a few days Pocahontas would help her mother and other relatives to plant number-three field, which would have ripe corn in what we call October. But every year, a big field was planted with corn that would be given to the great chief, as tribute (a sort of taxes). And today her father's field had to be planted — while he watched.

Powhatan had arrived at the village the afternoon before. He did not come alone. Very important people do not travel alone; they travel with groups of servants and hangers-on. Powhatan had traveled with several bodyguards — very tall, strong men; also with some of his wise men and with a few of his wives. (Pocahontas's mother had once been one of these. She felt no jealousy, for she knew that these women were just as temporary in Powhatan's life as she had been.)

Powhatan's coming had been greeted with great ceremony. The chief of the village and his wise men had sat on mats in front of the chief's longhouse. Powhatan and his followers had walked to meet him, dressed richly in many deerskins and wearing jewelry of shell, copper, and pearls. The people of the village had lined up on both sides of the way, shouting and singing their welcome. After the great chief had sat down facing the village chief, two of the village's wise men had greeted him formally with long, flattering speeches. Then a huge quantity of food — hours in the making, by the village's women including Pocahontas's mother — had been brought for a feast. After they had eaten, Powhatan and the village chief had smoked a pipe of tobacco together as a token of friendship. Indian tobacco was much stronger than ours. So only important people smoked it, and they did not smoke much of it at any one time. Then the villagers, men and women alike, had danced for a long time to entertain and honor Powhatan. (The dance was a very active, exciting one, almost like a war dance.) Finally, late in the evening, Powhatan and his followers had gone to bed, sleeping in a house specially set aside for them.

Indian town scene, with fishnets hung up

This morning Powhatan and his followers ate a big, luxurious breakfast. Their meal consisted of raw oysters and freshly roasted wild turkey. Then the guests and most of the villagers went to the big field that had been cleared for Powhatan's benefit. (A few men went hunting instead, so that there would be deer and more wild turkey to eat that evening.) Pocahontas and her relatives and neighbors carried digging sticks to poke holes in the ground. These holes were made about three feet apart. Pocahontas dropped in a few corn kernels and a few beans, and then she filled the hole up. (Her people did not use fish or anything else as fertilizer. That was why they had to keep shifting to newer fields each year.) Four months later, all the people of the village would harvest that field's corn. They would dry it, shell it from the cobs, put the kernels in baskets, and send the baskets by canoe to Powhatan's capital town. There it would be stored in the town's temple, along with the corn from the other villages the great chief ruled.

When the planting was all done, Powhatan walked backwards around the field, throwing presents of beads to the villagers. For special people, like Pocahontas and her mother, he would hand them the beads instead of throwing them. Then he and his followers went back to the village and rested before the evening's feast. The village women got busy with pounding up cornmeal in mortars and roasting the meat the men had brought in, while the men and boys went out to the fish trap for more fish.

This afternoon was the time when Pocahontas had a chance to visit with her father. He was a busy man, talking politics with the village chief. At sixty years of age, he was very old by Indian standards. And he was dignified and downright fearsome much of the time, as a good chief should be. But he had a soft spot for his wives (and ex-wives) and children. So of course he made some time to talk with his daughter and his former wife. That night, after the prayers and tobacco offerings were made at sunset, there was another feast, followed by dancing. The next morning Powhatan went home again, and Pocahontas did not see him again for a long time.

CHAPTER FIVE
A GIRL'S DAY IN LATE SUMMER

On a baking-hot day in late summer, the harvest season, Pocahontas was up before dawn. With her relatives she took a welcome bath in the river, for the heat and humidity were already high. The morning prayers were thankful, for the corn crop was a good one this year. After everyone who was hungry had eaten, the family members went out on their various errands. The men and boys were hunting and fishing as usual that day. Some of the women went out into the forest for more firewood. The other women planned to harvest some corn before the worst heat of the day came, and Pocahontas went along with them.

Number-one field had produced well and number-two field was beginning to do the same. This morning Pocahontas and her mother went out and picked the whatever ears of corn were fully ripe. After carrying them back to the village in baskets on their backs, they shucked the husks off and put the ears out to dry. In a couple of days they would shell the dried kernels from the cobs and put them back in the baskets to be stored inside the house.

Pocahontas and her mother and aunt finished their work in the field before the day became really hot. Back at the village, they dipped into the bubbling stewpot before turning to more tasks. Her mother went out in the canoe with her sisters-in-law to dig potting clay from a creekbank several miles away. While they were out, they also gathered the wild rice that was growing among the tuckahoe by now. Pocahontas stayed in the village to watch a couple of other women making pots from the clay they had dug several days earlier.

The women had picked the stones and leaves out of the clay, added crushed oyster shell to it, and then wrapped it carefully to keep moist until they had part of a day free. Now they each took a handful of clay and patted it into a "cone shape" for the pot's bottom. (Virginia Indian pots had pointed bottoms, so they could be pushed down amongst the embers of the fire. The Indians did not have stoves like ours.) Then the potters took another handful and rolled it into a "snake," which they pressed onto the rim of the "cone." After smoothing over the "valley" between "snake" and "cone," they rolled another "snake" and added that on. As more rolls were added, the sides of the pot grew.   It was slow, careful work because the pots had to be solid. After drying for a day or two, the pots would be laid upon some firewood, covered over with more wood and sticks, and heated very hot to make them tough. Sometimes pots broke during this "firing," and the woman's work

Rolling a fillet to add to the pot's bottom, during pottery-making

would be for nothing. So Pocahontas learned an important lesson: make things patiently and carefully so that they last.

That evening, after family prayers and tobacco offerings, and while her relatives dipped into the stewpot or ate the roasted and smoked fish that one of her uncles had brought in, Pocahontas listened to the adults exchanging news. She noticed that their hands were never still. The men were always repairing old hunting or fishing gear or making new things. Her grandfather, now suffering from arthritis (he was a little over forty years old, old for an Indian of that time), carved the wooden dishes for the family. And her mother and aunts were usually rolling string and twine from hemp they had gathered and dried. (Indians made their own string; there were no stores in those days where they could buy it.) People always needed twine and string — to make net bags that held berries, for instance. In fact, making twine long ahead of time was a necessity of life for the Indians. Once you made twine, you could make mats, and once you had mats you could cover a new house. This was a second important

Twisting twine by hand, Indian-style

lesson for Pocahontas: make simple things ahead of time, for you will need them later to make complicated things.

That night, the mosquitoes and gnats were out in force. Virginia is a very buggy place in the summertime. So in spite of the heat, Pocahontas and her family slept inside their house with the doors closed. The smoke from the fire in the center aisle kept all those insects out.

CHAPTER SIX
A GIRL'S DAY IN LATE FALL

On a crisp day in late fall, Pocahontas woke up in a house that was not in her family's village at all. It was far out in the woods, miles away from home. It was really in a camp, which would be moved that day.

After the last of the corn and beans and squash had been harvested, there had been a big thanksgiving ceremony. The whole village rejoiced in a good crop year. Then immediately afterward, in what we call October, the women and children and even some of the men had gone out into the forest every day to gather nuts. There were hickory nuts, walnuts, and chestnuts that could be eaten raw. There were also many kinds of acorns, which tasted bitter until they were soaked in water several times. Pocahontas's relatives dried most of these nuts and stored them in baskets, to eat during the winter.

Now it was the time of the great deer hunt. Whole families left the village and journeyed westward, where there were fewer people and more deer. The men planned to kill as many deer as they could, and the families would bring back the hides and the meat. The meat had to be dried during the trip before it spoiled. So there was much work for the women and children as well as the men.

There was also some real danger in taking this trip. The area they were going to was either near or on land claimed by the Monacan Indians. These people lived west of Powhatan's people and were usually unfriendly. They did not like people coming and hunting anywhere near their land.

This morning Pocahontas, her family, and a neighbor family all bathed briefly in the small stream they had camped beside. Then they prayed and offered tobacco, asking for a good hunt. They also prayed that no one that day would be bitten by a poisonous snake. They had brought snakeroot with them, but it might not be enough. And finally they asked that the Monacan Indians stay far away from them. Everyone who was hungry ate some food left over from last night. Afterward the men decided where they would hunt that day and arranged with the women where that night's camp would be set up.

The men and boys walked several miles, then fanned out and surrounded a large area where they thought a deer herd would be. Lighting fires and making noise, they slowly closed in toward the center of the circle. (Even the little boys helped with this.) Sure enough, there were 10 deer within the circle. These they killed with their bows and arrows. Then they gutted the carcasses and carried them toward the place where the new camp was to be.

Meanwhile Pocahontas and her mother, aunts, and girl cousins began to take apart the camp houses as soon as the men left. These houses were smaller than the ones in the village, because they had to be taken apart and put back together every day. First the women and girls unlashed the mats from the framework; then they unlashed the framework itself. In less than two hours, the houses were just bundles of saplings and mats, ready for carrying. Some of the women carried these house-makings. Other women and the girls carried cooking pots, wooden mortars for pounding corn they had brought, and the baskets that were filling up with partly treated deer hides and meat.

They walked with these burdens for about ten miles, along stream beds that wandered underneath tall oak and chestnut trees that had shed their leaves by now. The underbrush under these giant trees was not too thick for a fairly easy passage. Sometimes a woman would put down her burden and go off to the side, to dig Indian cucumber roots or to gather fruits like pawpaws, wild grapes, and sparkleberries, which the family would eat that night.

Deep forest, dark enough that fewer vines and bushes grow on the ground

Finally Pocahontas and her relatives arrived at the place chosen for the next camp. Like the other camp, it lay beside a small stream, so that there would be water nearby. The women and girls strung cords between several trees and hung out the partly dried deer meat they had carried, so that it could dry some more in the afternoon air. Then they began putting up the houses, which took nearly two hours. They had almost finished this job when the attack came.

Six Monacan men suddenly sprang into the camp, whooping fearsomely. They were painted for war and armed with bows and arrows. Seeing only women and girls, they quickly put away their weapons. In those days Indian warriors rarely killed women and children; instead they tried to grab them and take them home, where they would be brainwashed. Women and girls who were treated kindly but firmly could become the mothers of warriors for the Monacans; the boys could grow up to become Monacan warriors. Many people captured by both the Monacans and the Powhatans eventually forgot their own people, and they joined their captors' families. So now the Monacan men wanted to kidnap at least a couple of girls. Even though the men did not know who her father was, Pocahontas was in very great danger.

There were about twenty women and older girls in the camp. But they were not easy for any enemies to catch. Indian women and girls were strong from all the hard physical work they did. They all had knives for doing that work, and they knew exactly how to use them. Once the women and older girls got over their first fright, and when they saw the Monacan men dragging off three children, they got mad. Running after the enemy men, whooping and yelling loudly themselves, they ganged up on the warriors and slashed at any parts of them they could reach. They managed to make the men let go of two of the girls, but the third child could not be rescued. A Monacan man managed to hoist her up on his shoulders and run with her (Monacan men were terrific runners, just like the Powhatans), and he got away into the woods too quickly. The other men soon gave up the fight and darted away, holding their bleeding wounds.

There was nothing else for Pocahontas and her mother, aunts, and cousins to do but finish putting up the houses. This they did while crying bitterly over the loss of the girl, who was Pocahontas's cousin. Still crying, they were pounding corn into meal for supper when Pocahontas's uncles and boy cousins came into camp with the ten deer they had killed. Hearing what had happened, the men were outraged, and they promised to rescue the girl and take revenge.

Meanwhile, there was little they or the women could do; dusk would fall soon. So the men helped the women with the skinning of the deer and the slicing of the meat. Supper, which was made up of roasted deer meat and ash-cakes made of cornmeal, was quiet that evening. There was no joking or visiting after supper, either, for everyone was grieving over the loss of the girl. The Monacans would not harm her. But she was far from her parents, captured by enemies.

CHAPTER SEVEN
A GIRL'S DAY IN WINTER

Pocahontas woke up in her warm bed at home on a bitter-cold winter morning. There had been an ice storm two days before. When she crawled out of the house's low door, all the trees and branches were coated in ice. She knew that when the sun came up, they would glitter beautifully.

The family bathed in the river, as they did every day. Today, of course, they had to break through fairly thick ice first. That ice would keep people from going out in canoes, for fish or any other thing. After they prayed and offered tobacco, everyone who was hungry ate what was left over in the stewpot.

Then some of the women set out into the forest for firewood. They were having to walk farther and farther every day to find it. One day in spring the family's house would have to be rebuilt in a place near the newest field, where there was more firewood nearby. The men and boys all went out to hunt, even though there was dried deer meat stored in the house. The other women started pounding a lot of corn and cracking a lot of nuts to make into "walnut milk." The meat had to be fresh and the other foods plentiful, for there were visitors in the village today.

Pocahontas's grandmother was sick, so everyone had gathered to see her cured. The uncles had failed to bring back the girl the Monacans had taken. The grandmother missed her badly. The uncles had caught a Monacan girl instead and had given her to the grandmother. That child was being well treated but carefully watched so she did not get away. But to the grandmother it was not quite the same. She was grieving for her grandchild and for her son who had been wounded trying to get his daughter back. A priest from another, larger village had come and cured the uncle's wound with herbs.

The grandmother had remained listless, wanting to lie on her bed in the house all day. Several days before, the priest had been called to come again, this time to do a sweathouse ceremony for her to give her more energy. Every village had a sweathouse. It was a low house with lots of mats over it to keep in the heat. Several stones were heated very hot and placed (with tongs made of sticks) in the central hearth. The inner bark from an oak tree was put over them. Then the grandmother and several other women took off their clothes and went inside. The priest closed the door after them. The house was like a sauna, and sweating cleansed the women's pores. After a while, the priest opened the door and threw some water on the rocks to make steam. He also threw some water on the women, who were getting faint with the heat. Finally, after a long time, the women left the house and ran into the river, where the family had broken the ice and bathed that morning. Great heat followed by great cold was supposed to make people well. Usually it did, but not this time. Pocahontas and her family were very worried about the grandmother, who seemed to be fading slowly away from them.

So the priest was called yet again. This time the word went out that the illness was a serious one, so all the kinfolk living in other villages came to help with the grandmother's curing if they possibly could. They had to come by walking along the trails that linked villages, since the rivers, where travel was easier, were frozen over. The grandmother was glad to see her daughters, who had married and moved away. Her one surviving brother also came (the other brother had been killed in war years before). None of her sisters was still living; they had died either in child-birth or from years of hard work.

Pocahontas's kinsmen felt that sick people should not be alone in their ill-ness; seeing everybody's concern was part of curing a patient. But Pocahontas, being just a little girl, wondered instead if maybe the people had gathered so that

Grandmother would be less afraid of the priest. This stern-faced man knew a great many things that no one else did. True, he had a wife and children, but he lived away from them most of the time. He had to look after the tribe's temple and all the things kept in it. Pocahontas knew little of what was there, but it was scary all the same. The man himself was middle-aged and wore a shaggy, short cape. He carried only a rattle with him today; herbs from the forest were not needed.

The priest crawled through the low door, into the house where the grand-mother lay on the ground near the fire. He took little notice of all the many family members sitting on the beds along the sides of the house. His eyes were only for the patient, and his manner was gentle. He called for water, which he threw over

Scene from a Powhatan curing ritual

himself. Then taking his rattle in one hand, he beat loudly on his own chest with his other hand, as though begging the gods for the patient's health. Then he rose slowly and circled the patient. He shook the rattle softly all up and down the grandmother's body. Then he sprinkled her with more water, while murmuring words that nobody understood. They sounded sacred and must have been a prayer. Then he accepted some shell beads from one of Pocahontas's uncles and left the house. The ceremony was done slowly and took a long time. After it was over, the grandmother said she felt much better. All the family rejoiced with her, and they feasted until late in the evening. And after that day, she got well.

CHAPTER EIGHT
GOING TO LIVE WITH HER FATHER

When she was an older girl, perhaps eight, Pocahontas went to live with her father, Powhatan. (That would have been in about 1603.) Her parents finally divorced, and her mother remarried. From now on, Pocahontas would see her mother only when she went visiting. That was not too often, for she was busy in her father's household.

Pocahontas went to live in the capital town of a powerful chief. For the next few years she would be surrounded with important people who were richly dressed. However, she was still a girl, so she dressed like one. She still wore no clothing most days. She could put on a deerskin cape on the coldest days. When important visitors came, though, she might dress in a deerskin apron or a dancing costume of green leaves around her middle. Her head was still shaved except for one long lock of hair at the back. She would go on looking like this until she was about 15, in 1610. All the other girls in the town, including her half-sisters, dressed and wore their hair the same way.

Pocahontas had grown into a strong, robust girl. All the physical work she had done in her mother's village had made her muscular and rather stocky in body. She remained that way, for she went on doing the same work most days in her father's town. She did not grow very tall, unlike many of her people. But she had a handsome face, with a clear coppery complexion. More important, she had snapping black eyes that showed how lively she was. Pocahontas was witty and liked to tease people. That is why her father stopped calling her "Amonute" and started calling her "Pocahontas," which means "little mischievous one."

Pocahontas needed to be handsome and witty if she wanted her father's

The only portrait made of Pocahontas during her lifetime: Simon Van Der Passe's engraving, winter of 1616-17. Courtesy Virginia Historical Society

attention. Powhatan was a powerful man, and therefore a very busy man. He had many cares. He was always surrounded by lots of people: bodyguards, councillors, a succession of wives, and many of his children. A little girl could get lost in the shuffle.

Pocahontas's father had to meet fairly often with the chiefs who ruled the various parts of his domain. Sometimes he went to their towns, which meant that he was away. (Little girls were not taken on important trips.) Powhatan had to decide whether to make war on his Indian enemies; in that year of 1603, at least one European ship visited his territory as well. War was dangerous, even if not many people got killed back then. Powhatan had to talk for a long time with councillors and priests before he made up his mind. He did the talking in his house, and little girls were not invited to listen.

Powhatan had to take part in ceremonies in the temple, for the welfare of his

Indian town scene, with a pole-and-mat shade for people to sit under and talk

people. He could enter temples along with the priests, which no one else could do.
The temple was a building much like the house Pocahontas lived in, but it was out
in the woods and hardly anyone was allowed to go into it. The bodies of dead chiefs
were kept there, along with the valuables owned by the present chief. Powhatan
used the temple as his treasure-house. The priests kept a fire burning there all the
time, in honor of the main god that the people believed in. This deity appeared to
the priests when they called him; Powhatan himself may have seen him, too. This
god was the one who ordered all good Indian men to wear their hair in a certain
way: the right side shaved, the left side long and done up in a knot, and a "Mohawk"
tuft of hair along the top. Powhatan wore his own hair this way.

Powhatan was nearly sixty years old when Pocahontas went to live with him.
He was tall and strong. He had a broad Indian face, graying hair, a thin gray beard,

and a "sour" expression on his face, showing that he had carried many cares in his life.

But while Powhatan was a busy man, he was gentle with his wives and children. He played favorites, though: he had a favorite wife (while she lived with him) and a favorite daughter (until she married). That meant that the wives competed with each other, and the children were in competition, too. And Powhatan had seen enough wives and children come and go that now he was hard to please. Yet among the children, Pocahontas soon stood out. In fact, she wrapped her old father around her finger — up to a point.

Most days were "ordinary" days. On these, Pocahontas and her step-mothers and step-sisters worked just like other women. They bathed and prayed along with the household, and then they went out from the town and did women's work.

Tidal creek, semi-salty, with reeds growing in it

Pocahontas was doing the same work as before. But now she was doing it with step-mothers who had only a mild interest in her. And she was doing it with step-sisters who wanted more of their father's attention. It was lucky that Pocahontas was used to working in groups of people and getting along with them. If she had not been able to do that, her father would have sent her away.

Pocahontas was old enough now to do the heavy work, too. She gathered firewood at all seasons of the year. She scraped deer hides and tanned them whenever it was needed. She was expected to do more in planting, weeding, and harvesting the fields. She also helped cut reeds on the nicer winter and spring days. She and some women would paddle a canoe upriver to a reedy marsh. There they would chop the long, dry reeds and tie them in big, heavy bundles. Then they brought the bundles home in the canoe and stored them in the house rafters until they were needed for making mats. Since Powhatan's town had many houses, there would be

Close-up of marsh with reeds that were used to make mats for Indian houses

many trips made to the marsh every winter, to get enough reeds to last the year.

But living in Powhatan's household had its advantages. The tribute corn that his subject villages raised came to Powhatan, and now Pocahontas could eat some of it. With all that corn coming in, Powhatan did not have to eat tuckahoe for part of the year, for his corn did not run out. He was able to feast people all year long. But whenever a feast was ordered, all the women of Powhatan's house — including Pocahontas and even his favorite wife — would have to get busy pounding corn kernels into meal. Of course, once the food was done, Pocahontas got to share in the feast, though she did not sit with the important women like her step-mothers. Feasts were diplomatic occasions, and proper respect and protocol had to be observed, even by the great chief's favorite daughter.

There were certain "polite" things that Powhatan's followers and wives did during any feast given for an important visitor, whether the visitor was an Indian or a European. They came to the feasting-place, having painted themselves red with puccoon (dye made from a red root) and put on bracelets and necklaces of pearls and copper pieces and shell beads. They washed their hands and sat down, the women being separated from the men (the children like Pocahontas sat elsewhere, off at a distance). Food was brought by less important people in the town; a few of the wives would serve the chief and his visitor. Each person ate from an individual wooden bowl (on other days, people ate from a stewpot or a large wooden platter laden with meat). The bowl would contain helpings of all the foods being served: deer meat, turkey meat, cornbread, and a shell with "walnut milk" in it. When people finished eating what they wanted, they set their dishes aside. Any food left in them was given to the poor people of the town. After the feast, the townspeople, including Powhatan's wives and also perhaps Pocahontas, would dance to honor the visitor.

Pocahontas may have been her father's favorite, but she was still a little girl. And she looked like one. In 1607, she was about eleven years old,* still far from looking like a woman. She may have been the apple of her father's eye, but she lived in a world in which adult males, the trained fighters, were the ones who dealt with foreigners, who could be dangerous. That was her situation when the English arrived.

* In late 1616 or early 1617, when her portrait was engraved during her stay in England, its Latin caption said she was "aged 21 years."

Replica of the <u>Godspeed</u> arriving

CHAPTER NINE
THE COMING OF THE ENGLISH AND CAPTAIN JOHN SMITH

The ships carrying the men from England arrived at Jamestown in April 1607. The newcomers soon showed that they were not really the visitors they claimed to be. Instead of setting up their timber-and-mud-daub houses in the open, they built a fort around their houses, which meant they were not very friendly. They had no women or children with them — like Indian men when they took to the warpath. The English would become violent whenever they thought the Indians might be making a hostile move — whether the Indians meant to be hostile or not.

Sailors on the <u>Godspeed</u> lowering their boat to come ashore

So Powhatan knew that his warriors had better deal with them, not his young daughter. No Englishman saw Powhatan himself until December. That was probably true for Pocahontas, too. If Powhatan kept Pocahontas safely near him, then she did not see any English until December 1607.

The first Englishman that Pocahontas ever saw was Captain John Smith. He was a captive of her father's people at the time. He was then nearly 28 years old, and a seasoned military man

Engraving of Captain John Smith.
Courtesy Virginia Historical Society

who had seen many parts of the world. He had already been tested by the holiest priests in Powhatan's domain. The priests had said that he was a friend of the Indians (they were mostly wrong). So when Smith was finally brought to Powhatan's town, Powhatan feasted him and treated him like an important visitor. Everyone else treated him like an object of curiosity.

Engraving from the 1620s of John Smith being saved by Pocahontas. Courtesy Virginia Historical Society

The story of Powhatan suddenly ordering Smith to be killed, but being rescued by Pocahontas, may not have happened exactly that way. John Smith only wrote the story down many years later, after Pocahontas had gone to England and become famous. Since the priests had already declared him a "good" man, Smith probably did not need rescuing. But some kind of testing of him may have happened. And Pocahontas may have watched it all from the sidelines.

John Smith became an adopted "son" of Powhatan's (and "brother" of Pocahontas's) and was released. After that, Powhatan sent people with food to the colonists. Pocahontas may have gone along on those trips, but it was her father, not she, who had the power to send food to foreigners. Pocahontas would just have gone along to see the English fort, and also to watch John Smith among his own people. At that time he was one of several leaders of the struggling colony.

In February 1608 Smith returned to Powhatan's capital town for several days. He came on a trading mission, bringing an English ship's captain and a number of soldiers. The people of Powhatan's capital greeted them as honored guests, with shouting, speechmaking, feasting, and dancing.

Pocahontas may have been allowed to watch Smith and her father talking. She certainly saw at this time that Smith was an important man among his own people, for there were times when he seemed to be giving the captain not only advice but even orders. Smith was also good at trading, something Indian people admired. There was a lot of hard bargaining, for Powhatan was no slouch at trading, either. Finally Smith got the corn he wanted from Powhatan for a few pounds of blue glass beads. Beads like that were new to the Indians, seeming very beautiful. Pocahontas probably saw to it that her father gave her some of them later.

In the following spring, though, things went sour. The English stayed in their fort instead of moving to a town close to Powhatan. That seemed unfriendly, after Powhatan had adopted Smith and invited him to move. Some of Powhatan's people began stealing English tools and shooting at English men when they got the chance. It is unlikely that Pocahontas was allowed to visit the fort at Jamestown during this time. Powhatan realized that the English knew by then that Pocahontas was his favorite child. It was too tempting for the English to decide to take her as a hostage, to make the Indians to leave them in peace.

Finally in the late spring of 1608, the English, led by John Smith, captured some Indian men, held them hostage, and would not let them go. That made Powhatan have Pocahontas go to Jamestown — with several men to guard her — to ask for the captives' release. Sending her to the unfriendly English was definitely a gesture of friendship. John Smith understood and released the captives to Pocahontas, making things more peaceful for a while.

Pocahontas visited the English fort many times after that. But she would never have gone alone: she was too valuable as a possible hostage. So Powhatan must have sent bodyguards with her each time. John Smith was never alone, either. He always saw her inside the crowded fort, surrounded by his own men. There was no chance for the two of them to take walks in the woods and talk privately, even if they had wanted to. And John Smith probably did not want to.

Pocahontas saw that John Smith was a "real man" by Indian standards. He was brave and daring on behalf of his people. He was a boaster, but he had real accomplishments to boast about. Being a European, he was exotic in Indian eyes and he owned some mysterious gadgets. He also "owned" (the colony really owned them) a lot of glass beads, which Indian people regarded as a sort of money. When he had been a captive in Powhatan's power, John Smith's self-centeredness had not been very visible. His fellow Englishmen saw it, though, and many of them did not like him. But Pocahontas became fond of him. She may have thought of him as an adopted brother, or she may have had a crush on him. No one really knows.

For his part, John Smith did not have much time for little girls, even one who was the favorite daughter of a powerful chief. He found her handsome face and lively manner attractive, but her childish, unclothed body and shaven head probably did not interest him much. (Even adult women do not seem to have interested him much. He never married a wife, and there is no record of his ever having a girlfriend.) Smith had much more pressing things on his mind. He had to deal with a strong native chief, and he had to keep his own people working when they did not want to. He already had about two full-time jobs. So sometimes he noticed Pocahontas, in a patronizing way, and he treated her with respect. But that is all.

Pocahontas spent the rest of her time on her visits playing with the English boys. She teased them into turning cartwheels with her all over the fort.

The English in Jamestown fort

If Pocahontas came to the English fort often, it may have been as a spy for her father. Relations were getting bad again between him and the English as the year 1608 went on. The English were doing things — things which took John Smith away from Jamestown during Pocahontas's visits — that angered Powhatan.

Smith and his men explored the Chesapeake Bay twice in the summer of 1608. Yet Powhatan felt that most of that region was his own territory. In the fall of 1608 John Smith's superiors tried to make better friends with Powhatan by coming to his capital town and "crowning" him. Pocahontas and the other girls danced for the Englishmen when they arrived. But the "crowning" was less than successful because Powhatan refused to kneel. Then Smith and some Englishmen went out toward the west and met the Monacans, Powhatan's enemies, against Powhatan's orders. Finally in January 1609, Smith and Powhatan met for trading, and each tried to ambush each other at the same time. Smith and his men's guns won the day, which made Powhatan furious. Smith had to spend most of the night in a capital town ruled by an angry chief, and he wrote later that the ever-loyal Pocahontas came to warn him that Powhatan would try to kill him. She did not really need to warn him; Smith was smart enough to know it by himself. But he did nothing to make peace with her father; rather the opposite. Instead he and his men went upriver, and at gunpoint they took most of the winter's stores of corn from the Indians there.

After that January falling-out, Powhatan moved to another capital town much farther away from Jamestown. As a young member of his household, Pocahontas would have had to move with him. After that, it would have been harder for her to visit the English fort, if she tried to visit at all. It would also have been more dangerous for her. The Indian men were sniping at any Englishman they could find, while the English became even more trigger-happy. In the summer of 1609, Smith was away from Jamestown a great deal, trying to set up more English settlements up and down the James River. The Indians at those places, Powhatan's subjects, were very angry at the intrusion. Blood was shed, and the settlements failed. John Smith, by then the main leader of the English, was the man who threatened Powhatan the most and who made the old man the most angry.

During that spring and summer of 1609, then, Pocahontas was caught between her father and her friend; but she probably saw little of the friend. Given the fighting that was going on, she would have had tremendous value as a hostage, and both she and her father must have known it. So if and when she went to the Jamestown fort at all, she went well guarded. And yet she kept her interest in, and some sympathy for, the English and her "brother" John Smith.

In September 1609, while he sailing down the James River to Jamestown, John Smith was seriously injured by a powder explosion. He had to leave for England shortly afterward to recover. Smith did not say goodbye to Pocahontas. He was not as greatly attached to her as she was to him. He saw her as a nice kid, but he was a very sick man when he left. So he did not even leave a message for her.

The next time Pocahontas came to the Jamestown fort, she found Smith

The fort, empty of John Smith's presence

missing. She became upset and asked what had happened to him. The Englishmen she asked felt sorry for her. Instead of telling her Smith had left without a word, they told her a lie: that he had been killed. After that, her visits, if she still made them, were fewer. The fort had lost a major attraction for her when Smith sailed away.

CHAPTER TEN
AFTER JOHN SMITH'S DEPARTURE

Pocahontas would not see Captain John Smith again until seven years later — and then she would be angry about that lie. A year or so after Smith left Virginia, Pocahontas became a woman with monthly periods. She put on an woman's deerskin apron and grew out her hair. She courted and married an Indian man named Kocoum and went to live with him in his village.

She did not expect to see any Englishmen again, especially John Smith, but  she was wrong. The English captured her in 1613 and kept her for a year. During that time she fell in love with John Rolfe, which meant divorcing Kocoum. (We do not know if she had any children by him.) Rolfe, who loved her in return, married her and took her and their son Thomas to England. There she saw John Smith again — but all of that is another story.

Couple paddling away in a dugout canoe, as Pocahontas and her Indian husband did in about 1611

ORDER FORM
YOUNG POCAHONTAS IN THE INDIAN WORLD

Please forward _____ copies of YOUNG POCAHONTAS IN THE INDIAN WORLD
See payment options listed below.

PREPAID

_____ books at $8.95 per copy   _____

Virginia sales tax at 4.5% per copy   _____

Shipping & Handling one book - $6.00.
    Shipping & Handling additional books
    to same destination $1.50 each   _____

Total enclosed   _____

COD
Per copy price and tax same as above, plus COD shipping costs.

SPECIAL/WHOLESALE
Delivery arrangements with purchase order can be made by contacting
J&R Graphic Services, Inc. via E-mail: susie@jrgraphics.com or
Fax (757) 595-2611.

Please make all checks payable to Helen C. Rountree.
Allow 4-6 weeks for delivery.

Ordered by: Ship to:

Name _____   Name _____

Address _____   Address _____

_____   _____

Please complete order form and send it to:

HELEN C. ROUNTREE
C/O J & R GRAPHIC SERVICES INC.
124 PRODUCTION DRIVE
YORKTOWN, VA 23693
Fax: (757) 595-2611 • E-MAIL: susie@jrgraphics.com